# Key to Using Prepositions and Particles

## WORKBOOKS
### ONE, TWO, AND THREE

*J. B. Heaton*

LONGMAN

**LONGMAN GROUP LIMITED**
London

*Associated companies, branches and representatives
throughout the world*

†*First published 1967*
*New impressions *1971; *1972; *1974;*
*\*1975; *1976 *1977; *1978 : *1979*

ISBN 0 582 52120 3

Filmset by Graphic Film Limited, Dublin, Ireland

*Printed in Hong Kong by
Wing Tai Cheung Printing Co. Ltd.*

# WORKBOOK ONE

## Exercise 1

*After, behind, over, under*

| | | |
|---|---|---|
| **1** over | **11** under | **20** after |
| **2** behind | **12** behind | **21** over |
| **3** under | **13** after | **22** behind |
| **4** behind | **14** under | **23** under |
| **5** over | **15** behind | **24** over |
| **6** over | **16** behind | **25** after |
| **7** under | **17** after | **26** over |
| **8** under ... over | **18** after ... behind | **27** over |
| **9** after | **19** under | **28** after |
| **10** behind | | |

## Exercise 2

*On, in, off*

| | | |
|---|---|---|
| **1** on | **7** on ... in | **12** off |
| **2** off | **8** on ... in | **13** in |
| **3** on | **9** in | **14** in ... on |
| **4** in | **10** off | **15** on |
| **5** on | **11** in | **16** on |
| **6** in ... on | | |

## Exercise 3

*Word order*

**1** ... written *by* Bernard Shaw

**2** ... early *at* the station

**3** ... hiding *among* the trees

**4** ... meeting *before* him

5 . . . slowly *down* the river

6 . . . flying *towards* the border

7 . . . lecture *except* John

8 . . . now *beyond* a joke

9 . . . here *around* five

10 . . . object *under* the surface

11 . . . hammered *on* the door

12 . . . talks *with* a Scottish

13 . . . painted *over* the sign

14 . . . flying *above* the door

15 . . . sleeping *behind* the chair

16 . . . jump *over* the gate

17 . . . was *beneath* his dignity

18 . . . coat *underneath* mine

19 . . . got *into* trouble

20 . . . busy *along* the railway-line

21 . . . here *for* twelve years

22 . . . flows *through* the town

23 . . . by *over* two hundred

24 . . . money *besides* many clothes

25 . . . do *during* the Easter

26 . . . been *near* us

27 . . . no one *but* his own son

28 . . . pen *for* the work

29 . . . travel *by* night

30 . . . sat *in front of* the fire

**Exercise 4**

*Prepositions easily confused*

| | | | | |
|---|---|---|---|---|
| **1** 3 | **4** 2 | **7** 1 | **9** 4 | **11** 11 |
| **2** 8 | **5** 7 | **8** 12 | **10** 10 | **12** 6 |
| **3** 5 | **6** 9 | | | |

**Exercise 5**

*After, before, during, until, by*

| | | |
|---|---|---|
| **1** after | **3** during | **5** until |
| **2** by | **4** before | **6** by . . . during |

| | | |
|---|---|---|
| **7** after | **14** after | **20** by |
| **8** before | **15** during | **21** during |
| **9** until | **16** after | **22** before |
| **10** by | **17** by | **23** by |
| **11** after ... until | **18** until | **24** by |
| **12** by | **19** after | **25** after |
| **13** during | | |

## Exercise 6

*To, at, in*

| | | |
|---|---|---|
| **1** in | **10** in | **19** in ... at |
| **2** to | **11** at | **20** in |
| **3** in | **12** at | **21** at |
| **4** at | **13** to | **22** to |
| **5** in | **14** in | **23** at ... in |
| **6** at | **15** at | ... in |
| **7** in | **16** at | **24** at |
| **8** to | **17** to | **25** in ... at |
| **9** in | **18** at | |

## Exercise 7

*Word order*

**1** ... teacher *for* the book

**2** ... jury *of* North's innocence

**3** ... him *from* duty

**4** ... the king *for* mercy

**5** ... money *between* her two sons

**6** ... winner *on* his success

**7** ... car *in* a nearby garage

**8** ... villagers *of* their goods

**9** ... boy *for* his offence

**10** ... pupil *in* the art of dancing

**11** ... candidates *in* physics

**12** ... us *to* the hotel

5

**13** . . . information *from* the detectives

**14** . . . him *with* my money

**15** . . . everyone *about* the recent argument

**16** . . . actions *to* him

## Exercise 8

*Prepositions introducing participle phrases*
(Use each phrase in column B once only.)

*How ?*
1 Mr Brown rewarded John by giving him some money.
2 He wants to punish the boys by refusing to see them.
3 Joan started her new job by arriving before the other workers.
4 We are preparing for the test by reading these books at home.

*Why?*
5 Lily apologised to us for being rude.
6 We thanked Mr Lee for taking us on the picnic.
7 Someone paid us for acting in the film.
8 He will not forgive Henry for his bad manners.

## Exercise 9

*From, of, by, with*

| | | | | |
|---|---|---|---|---|
| 1 of | 5 by | 9 from | 13 with | 17 of |
| 2 by | 6 with | 10 by | 14 by | 18 from |
| 3 with | 7 of | 11 of | 15 from | 19 with |
| 4 from | 8 with | 12 by | 16 of | 20 of |

| 21 by | 23 from | 25 of | 27 with | 28 of |
|-------|---------|-------|---------|-------|
| 22 with | 24 with | 26 with | | |

## Exercise 10

*Below, under, above, over*

| 1 under | 11 under | 21 below |
|---------|----------|----------|
| 2 over | 12 over | 22 over |
| 3 below | 13 under | 23 under |
| 4 over | 14 over | 24 under |
| 5 above | 15 above | 25 over |
| 6 above | 16 below | 26 above |
| 7 over(across) | 17 over | 27 over |
| 8 under | 18 above | 28 under |
| 9 below | 19 under | 29 under |
| 10 over . . . above | 20 over | 30 over |

## Exercise 11

*Direct and indirect objects*

1 Throw the ball to me.
2 Did he offer a cigarette to you?
3 No, but he gave one to Tom.
4 Please bring me the glass.
5 The old man paid a lot of money to the doctor.
6 I read the blind man the letter.
7 'Have you left a piece of cake for your brother?' Peter's mother asked.
8 'I owe you a lot: you saved my life,' I told him.
9 Can anyone lend a pen to me? My sister is using mine.
10 The teacher showed Mr Smart Jack's untidy work.

11 Save me a seat, please!
12 She bought a new dress for herself.
13 Mr Jones denied nothing to his daughter.
14 Hand a pencil to me if you can spare one.
15 My friend at the theatre got me the ticket.

**Exercise 12**

*Combinations with* TO BE
(Use each word or phrase once only.)

| | | |
|---|---|---|
| **1** in | **5** off | **8** out |
| **2** with | **6** up to | **9** about to |
| **3** after | **7** out of | **10** on |
| **5** off | | |

**Exercise 13**

*Prepositions easily confused*

| | | | | |
|---|---|---|---|---|
| **1** at | **4** between | **7** for | **10** over | **12** on |
| **2** below | **5** about | **8** besides | **11** in | **13** over |
| **3** above | **6** with | **9** under | | |

**Exercise 14**

*For, since*

| | | | | |
|---|---|---|---|---|
| **1** for | **5** since | **9** since | **13** For | **17** since |
| **2** for | **6** for | **10** for | **14** Since | **18** for |
| **3** for | **7** since | **11** since | **15** for | **19** for |
| **4** since | **8** for | **12** for | **16** since | **20** since |

**Exercise 15**

*When? and Where?*

1 He was born in 1936.
2 He was born in Nairobi.
3 He lived in Nairobi for ten years.
4 He went to England in 1946.
5 Winbury is in Essex, England.
6 He lived in Nairobi (at 26 Gladstone Avenue, Nairobi,) before 1946.
7 He lived in England after 1946.
8 He was in Nairobi during the 1939–1945 war.
9 He spent three years at London University.
10 He left the university in 1957.
11 It was in Edinburgh.
12 It is now (ten, eleven, twelve, etc.) years since his graduation.
13 He went to Italy in 1961.
14 It is now (six, seven, eight, etc.) years since his arrival in Italy.
15 He has been living in Italy for (six, seven, eight, etc.) years.
16 He was married in 1962.
17 He is now living in Rome.
18 He will have lived in Italy for thirteen years by 1974.

**Exercise 16**

*Prepositional phrases*

| | | | | |
|---|---|---|---|---|
| 1 C | 3 B | 4 B | 5 D | 6 X |
| 2 A | | | | |

## Exercise 17

*Prepositions denoting Time*

| | | | | |
|---|---|---|---|---|
| **1** at | **4** In | **7** in | **10** in | **13** X |
| **2** in | **5** at | **8** at | **11** X | **14** in |
| **3** at | **6** in | **9** at | **12** on | |

## Exercise 18

*Single prepositions*

| | | |
|---|---|---|
| **1** with | **9** against | **17** towards |
| **2** under | **10** for | **18** with |
| **3** to | **11** through(by) | **19** around |
| **4** over | **12** in | **20** of |
| **5** without | **13** against | **21** by |
| **6** with | **14** after | **22** besides |
| **7** about(on) | **15** between | **23** by(with) |
| **8** after | **16** but | **24** beyond |

## Exercise 19

*Prepositions denoting Time*

| | | |
|---|---|---|
| **1** at | **7** in | **13** since |
| **2** in | **8** since | **14** during |
| **3** at | **9** for ... by | **15** from ... to |
| **4** since | **10** after | (until) |
| **5** in | **11** at | **16** until |
| **6** by | **12** for | |

## Exercise 20

*Prepositions denoting Place and Motion*

| | |
|---|---|
| 1 in | 21 to |
| 2 on (at, near) | 22 towards (for) |
| 3 above | 23 from |
| 4 in | 24 for (to) |
| 5 at (in) | 25 against (on) |
| 6 on | 26 to (at) |
| 7 up | 27 through (down, up) |
| 8 in | 28 to |
| 9 in (inside) | 29 for |
| 10 at | 30 by (near) |
| 11 in | 31 at |
| 12 at | 32 off (from) |
| 13 on (in) | 33 off (from) |
| 14 below | 34 through |
| 15 out of (outside) | 35 from |
| 16 in | 36 from |
| 17 behind (up) | 37 off |
| 18 in | 38 at |
| 19 in | 39 down |
| 20 on | 40 by |

## Exercise 21

*Single prepositions*

| | |
|---|---|
| 1 about | 6 with |
| 2 by | 7 except (but, save) |
| 3 through | 8 beneath |
| 4 to | 9 with |
| 5 without | 10 Throughout |

11 within (in, after)
12 but (except, save)
13 of
14 through (into, at)
15 near (at)
16 with
17 on (about)
18 among (amongst, through)
19 round (in)
20 of
21 with . . . since
22 During
23 for
24 in
25 between
26 By
27 for (besides, with)

28 of
29 over (past, about)
30 by (past)
31 in
32 for
33 under (for)
34 through . . . from (onto, over)
35 since (from)
36 among (in)
37 to (towards)
38 for
39 among (amongst, with)
40 until
41 by (before)
42 under (with)

**Exercise 22**

*Single prepositions*

1 at
2 on
3 to
4 through
5 from
6 in
7 of
8 to (towards, for, through)
9 with
10 in
11 after

12 for
13 by
14 in (inside)
15 on
16 On
17 for
18 on
19 about (on)
20 about
21 without

**Exercise 23**

*Phrases* (MODEL ANSWER)

Last Tuesday, John Lee and I decided to go to Smith-town. 'How shall we go?' asked John. 'Let's go *by train*,' I replied. We *arrived at* the station at 9.30 to catch the 9.40 train. A large notice board informed us that the train for Smithtown would *depart from* Platform 2, *calling at* several other places on the way. The train came in *on time* and we *got on*, found a comfortable compartment and settled down to read the newspapers which, *together with* some magazines, we had bought at the station bookstall. When we reached Smithtown, we realised that we had seen no more of the countryside than if we had been travelling *by night*.

**Exercise 24**

*Up*

| | | |
|---|---|---|
| 1 Count | 8 Cheer | 15 Eat |
| 2 tore | 9 fill | 16 mixed |
| 3 polished | 10 ended | 17 tidy |
| 4 summoned | 11 cleared | 18 chopped |
| 5 booked | 12 bought | 19 Drink |
| 6 dig | 13 Hurry | 20 saving |
| 7 blew | 14 pack | |

**Exercise 25**

*Out*

| | | |
|---|---|---|
| 1 died | 3 miss | 5 smoothing |
| 2 spit | 4 find | 6 wash |

| | | |
|---|---|---|
| 7 reason | 12 crowded | 17 helped |
| 8 rubbed | 13 picked | 18 Empty |
| 9 knocked | 14 tried | 19 give |
| 10 carry | 15 faded | 20 worn |
| 11 bail | 16 hear | |

## Exercise 26

*Adverbial particles*

| | |
|---|---|
| 1 off | 12 off |
| 2 by (past) | 13 along (round, around, |
| 3 in | over) |
| 4 up | 14 about (around) |
| 5 up | 15 in |
| 6 over | 16 on |
| 7 round | 17 out (up) |
| 8 over | 18 behind |
| 9 up | 19 over |
| 10 away | 20 out (outside) |
| 11 about (around) | |

## Exercise 27

*Replacement: prepositional phrases*

| | | |
|---|---|---|
| 1 in suspense | 7 at hand | 13 at best |
| 2 at present | 8 on record | 14 in the long |
| 3 in demand | 9 under pressure | run |
| 4 to his face | 10 under the sun | 15 in the clouds |
| 5 in cold blood | 11 by chance | |
| 6 in any case | 12 in place | |

**Exercise 28**

*The same noun in different phrases* (MODEL ANSWERS)

**1a** The big boy couldn't go half fare on the bus because he was *over age*.
 **b** You shouldn't smoke yet: you're *under age*.

**2a** Victory was *in the air* and everyone was beginning to rejoice.
 **b** 'Did you hear the President *on the air* last night?' 'No, I haven't a radio.'

**3a** Don't worry: the mistake you made is *of no account*.
 **b** *On no account* must you go out during this typhoon: it is very dangerous.

**4a** Mrs Lee is very *up to date* in the clothes she wears: she is very fashionable.
 **b** This map is *out of date*: many changes have been made since it was drawn.

**5a** The ship will sail as soon as all the passengers are *on board*.
 **b** All Mr Jones's actions are *above board*: everyone knows how honest he is.

**Exercise 29**

*Replacement: single words for prepositional phrases*

| | | |
|---|---|---|
| **1** free | **4** willingly (freely) | **7** mad (insane) |
| **2** outside | **5** punctually | **8** exactly |
| **3** burning | **6** immediately | |

## Exercise 30

*Missing preposition + noun*

| | | | | |
|---|---|---|---|---|
| 1 by | 5 In | 9 in | 13 in | 17 on |
| 2 on | 6 in | 10 in | 14 at | 18 in |
| 3 in | 7 on | 11 by | 15 at | 19 in |
| 4 by | 8 on | 12 off | 16 in | 20 on |

## Exercise 31

*Prepositional phrases from given nouns*

| | | |
|---|---|---|
| 1 in public | 8 for sale | 15 at home |
| 2 out of work | 9 in anger | 16 at (in) the office |
| 3 in debt | 10 in harmony | |
| 4 on the air | 11 in secret | 17 on purpose |
| 5 by bus | 12 out of danger | 18 by ship |
| 6 in case | 13 in ink | 19 in spring |
| 7 on fire | 14 on the way | 20 to plan |

## Exercise 32

*Prepositional phrases containing the noun* TIME(S)

| | |
|---|---|
| 1 . . . to time | 7 . . . *will solve the problem* in time |
| 2 At times . . . | |
| 3 . . . at that time | 8 . . . in time |
| 4 . . . for the time being | 9 . . . *old friends* from time to time |
| 5 . . . before my time | |
| 6 . . . in his time (during his lifetime) | 10 . . . *on the spot* in no time (in less than no time) |

**Exercise 33**

*Nouns followed by prepositions*

| | | |
|---|---|---|
| **1** of | **11** for | **21** to (into) |
| **2** for | **12** in | **22** of |
| **3** of | **13** in | **23** for |
| **4** on (about) | **14** to (towards) | **24** for |
| **5** of | **15** from | **25** for |
| **6** between | **16** for | **26** of |
| **7** to | **17** to | **27** over |
| **8** to | **18** in | **28** to |
| **9** with | **19** for | **29** of |
| **10** on (upon) | **20** for | **30** in |

**Exercise 34**

*Adjectives followed by prepositions*

| | | |
|---|---|---|
| **1** from | **11** to | **21** to |
| **2** to | **12** for | **22** to |
| **3** of (about) | **13** to | **23** of |
| **4** from (to) | **14** to | **24** to |
| **5** at (by) | **15** with | **25** for |
| **6** in | **16** for | **26** to |
| **7** of (about) | **17** of | **27** of (about) |
| **8** of | **18** in | **28** to |
| **9** to | **19** of | **29** to |
| **10** to | **20** of | **30** of (about) |

**Exercise 35**

*Verbs followed by prepositions*

| | | |
|---|---|---|
| **1** for | **3** in | **5** to |
| **2** on (upon) | **4** for | **6** from |

17

| | | |
|---|---|---|
| 7 to | 14 at | 20 from |
| 8 of (about) | 15 at | 21 about (over) |
| 9 at | 16 with | 22 for |
| 10 to (with) | 17 to | 23 for |
| 11 about | 18 at | 24 for (with) |
| 12 to | 19 for | 25 on (upon) |
| 13 about (of) | | |

## Exercise 36

*Verbs and adjectives followed by prepositions*

| | | |
|---|---|---|
| 1 for | 8 from | 15 to |
| 2 from | 9 for | 16 at |
| 3 in | 10 at | 17 on (upon) |
| 4 at | 11 from | 18 with |
| 5 in | 12 to | 19 from |
| 6 in | 13 at | 20 on |
| 7 at (in) | 14 of | |

## Exercise 37

*Prepositional phrases containing the noun* MIND(S)

| | |
|---|---|
| 1 ... in two minds | 4 ... in his right mind |
| 2 To my mind ... | 5 ... of a (one) mind |
| 3 ... out of his mind | 6 Keep in mind ... |

## Exercise 38

*Verbs followed by prepositions*   (MODEL ANSWERS)

approve *of*   The old man does not *approve of* women smoking.

18

believe *in*     Many people still believe in their grandmothers' old-fashioned remedies.

depart *from*     Your train will *depart from* Platform 5.

depend *on*     You cannot *depend on* Jack Bloggs: he is most unreliable.

listen *for*     I *listened for* the sound of footsteps but I could not hear anything.

prevent *from*     Tom's father *prevented* him *from* going on the picnic by making him clean the car and tidy up the garden.

recover *from*     Ann visited me as soon as she had *recovered from* her illness.

rely *on*     You can *rely on* me. I shall always try to help you.

supply *to*     The army *supplied* rifles *to* the peasants and told them to defend their villages.

trust *with*     The spy did not want to *trust* anyone *with* the valuable information.

## Exercise 39

*Phrasal verbs*

give up = surrender
look down upon = scorn
try out = test
head off = intercept
go off = explode

fall through = fail
do away with = abolish
turn down = reject
draw out = prolong
sit back = relax

## Exercise 40

*Word order: phrasal verbs*

1 ... held *it* up
2 ... give *it* up

3 ... taken *it* up
4 ... carry *them* out

5 . . . draw *it* up
6 . . . look *him* (*her*) up
7 . . . drew *it* out
8 . . . had *him* (*her*) up
9 Pack *them* up . . .
10 . . . called *him* up

11 . . . brought *it* up
12 . . . made *it* up
13 . . . let *it* out
14 . . . took *it* up
15 . . . back *him* up

## Exercise 41

*Phrasal verbs*

1 discovered
2 delayed
3 leave
4 stop
5 returns
6 invent

7 Complete
8 intercept *the others at* . . .
9 escaped
10 revise
11 understand
12 distributed

## Exercise 42

*Phrasal verbs*

1 called off
2 give away
3 running over
4 brought about
5 take off *your hat
and coat* (take
*your hat and coat*
off)

6 showing off
7 getting on
8 put up with
9 work out
10 make out
11 called up *his secretary*
(called *his secretary* up)
12 keep back

**Exercise 43**

*Word order: phrasal verbs and verbs followed by prepositions*

1 Look after *him* . . .
2 . . . stay with *her*
3 . . . tie *it* up
4 . . . preparing for *it*
5 . . . take *it* off
6 . . . jumped off *it*

7 . . . took to *him (her)*
8 . . . decided on *it*
9 . . . asked *them* in
10 . . . made *it* up
11 . . . going in for *it*
12 . . . get on with *them*

**Exercise 44**

*Go*

1 spread
2 sank
3 accompanying
4 approached
5 descended
6 entered
7 leaving

8 ascend
9 returned
10 passes
11 started
12 exceeded
13 match
14 explain

15 examined
16 happening
17 explode
18 attacked
19 is contrary to
20 Make an attempt at

**Exercise 45**

*Get*

1 got off
2 get on
3 get over
4 got up
5 get round
6 get on (along, by)

7 get away (out)
8 got at
9 got in
10 get over
11 got through

12 got up
13 getting at
14 get through
15 getting on (along)

21

**Exercise 46**

*Look*

| | | |
|---|---|---|
| 1 investigating | 6 find | 11 visit *my old friend* |
| 2 regarded | 7 respected | 12 improving |
| 3 take care of | 8 resemble | 13 relied on |
| 4 remember | 9 hope for | 14 scorned |
| 5 Be careful | 10 examined | |

**Exercise 47**

*Miscellaneous*

| | | |
|---|---|---|
| 1 with | 9 at | 17 on (upon) |
| 2 about (over) | 10 at | 18 to |
| 3 between | 11 with | 19 over |
| 4 In | 12 out | 20 At |
| 5 from | 13 out of | 21 without |
| 6 to | 14 to | 22 to |
| 7 at | 15 in | 23 at |
| 8 of (about) | 16 at | 24 in |

**Exercise 48**

*Miscellaneous*

| | | |
|---|---|---|
| 1 from | 7 for | 13 After (In) |
| 2 out (off) | 8 in | 14 in |
| 3 in | 9 up | 15 out |
| 4 of | 10 against | 16 at |
| 5 X | 11 by | 17 before |
| 6 of | 12 for | 18 into |

19 like
20 on (upon)
21 for
22 out
23 beyond
24 on (upon)
25 off

26 on (upon)
27 of
28 up
29 of
30 on
31 for

32 back
33 of
34 for
35 by
36 to
37 X

# WORKBOOK TWO

## Exercise 1

*Prepositional phrases*

| | | |
|---|---|---|
| **1** at | **7** in | **12** beyond |
| **2** by | **8** under | **13** between |
| **3** on | **9** on | **14** by |
| **4** on | **10** off | **15** all |
| **5** by | **11** for | **16** on |
| **6** in | | |

## Exercise 2

*Verbs, nouns and adjectives followed by prepositions*

| | | | | | | | | | |
|---|---|---|---|---|---|---|---|---|---|
| **1** 2 | | **9** 13 | **17** 19 | **25** 30 (29) | **33** 35 |
| **2** 6 | | **10** 16 | **18** 21 | **26** 29 (30) | **34** 37 |
| **3** 5 | | **11** 15 | **19** 24 | **27** 31 | **35** 39 |
| **4** 1 | | **12** 9 | **20** 17 | **28** 26 | **36** 38 |
| **5** 8 | | **13** 14 | **21** 23 | **29** 25 | **37** 33 |
| **6** 3 | | **14** 11 | **22** 18 | **30** 27 | **38** 36 |
| **7** 4 | | **15** 10 | **23** 20 | **31** 32 | **39** 40 |
| **8** 7 | | **16** 12 | **24** 22 | **32** 28 | **40** 34 |

## Exercise 3

*Verbs followed by prepositions*

| | | |
|---|---|---|
| **1** from | **5** from | **9** from |
| **2** against (from) | **6** of | **10** on |
| **3** with (to) | **7** from | **11** with |
| **4** from | **8** with | **12** for |

## Exercise 4

*Phrases including* TO

| | | |
|---|---|---|
| 1 prior | 5 Next | 8 due |
| 2 Owing | 6 next | 9 as |
| 3 According | 7 prior | 10 according |

## Exercise 5

*For, since*

1 Ann has been waiting for Tom *since* six o'clock.
2 We've been swimming *for* half an hour.
3 Mrs Lee has been crying *since* John's departure.
4 Has Alfred met you *since* last week?
5 Henry has been working very hard *since* last September.
6 He's not smoked any cigarettes *for* seven months.
  OR He's not smoked any cigarettes *since* the beginning of this year.
7 I've been listening to Mr White *for* two hours.
8 We've been playing tennis *since* early this morning.
9 I've been walking *since* dawn.
10 Miss Smith has been working as the manager's secretary *for* eight years.

## Exercise 6

*Word order: verbs followed by prepositions and phrasal verbs*

| | |
|---|---|
| 1 . . . answer for *them* | 4 . . . make *it* out |
| 2 . . . hard for *him* to live *it* down | 5 . . . figure *it* out |
| 3 Hand *it* over | 6 . . . go *into* it |
| | 7 Keep off *it* |

  8 'Keep *it* off'
  9 . . . put *them* up
10 . . . gave *it* away
11 . . . had *it* on
12 . . . happened on *them*
13 . . . come under *it*
14 . . . bear with *him*

15 . . . bears *it* out
16 . . . throw *it* up
17 . . . taken with *it*
18 . . . is up against *it*
19 . . . is given to *them*
20 . . . made off with *it* (all)

## Exercise 7

*Adverbial particles*

  1 out
  2 in
  3 up
  4 over (down)
  5 off (down) . . .
  6 round
  7 up
  8 up
  9 out
10 out
11 on
12 over
13 down
14 out
15 behind
16 on
17 out
18 on (up)
19 on . . . on
20 away (off)
21 up
22 up
23 round (around)
24 over
25 out (through)
26 on
27 in
28 away (off)
29 down (along)
30 behind (off)
31 back (aside)
32 away
33 out
34 away
35 by (past)
36 down

## Exercise 8

*Off, out, up*

  1 off
  2 out
  3 out
  4 up . . . out
  5 up
  6 out
  7 off
  8 up
  9 up
10 up
11 out . . . off
12 out . . . out

| 13 up | 17 out | 20 out |
|---|---|---|
| 14 out | 18 up | 21 up |
| 15 off (away) | 19 off | 22 up |
| 16 up | | |

## Exercise 9

*Get*

| 1 escaped | 13 depressing me |
|---|---|
| 2 return | 14 leaving (running away) |
| 3 hinting at (implying, driving at) | 15 teasing (poking fun at) |
| | 16 manage |
| 4 recovered from | 17 evade |
| 5 bribe | 18 enter (break into) |
| 6 concentrate on (attend to) | 19 finished (used up, eaten) |
| 7 mounted | 20 stole (took) |
| 8 reached (arrived at) | 21 cover (cover up) |
| 9 spread to | 22 arive at (reach) |
| 10 approaching | 23 arranged (organised) |
| 11 was friendly with | 24 going (leaving) |
| 12 stood up (rose to her feet) | |

## Exercise 10

*In spite of*

## Exercise 11

*In/on/by/at/with/for/under/to + noun + preposition*

*In*

| 1 of | 2 of | 3 to | 4 with | 5 of |
|---|---|---|---|---|

| | | | | |
|---|---|---|---|---|
| **6** to | **8** of | **10** of | **11** of | **12** for (to) |
| **7** of | **9** for | | | |

*On*

| | | | | |
|---|---|---|---|---|
| **13** with | **15** of | **17** of | **19** with | **20** of |
| **14** of | **16** with | **18** of | | |

*By*

| | | | |
|---|---|---|---|
| **21** of | **22** of | **23** of | **24** of |

*At*

| | | | | |
|---|---|---|---|---|
| **25** of | **27** of | **28** on (upon) | **29** of | **30** with |
| **26** with | | | | |

*With*

| | | | |
|---|---|---|---|
| **31** to | **32** to | **33** of | **34** to |

*For*

| | |
|---|---|
| **35** of | **36** of |

*Under*

| | | | |
|---|---|---|---|
| **37** of | **38** of | **39** of | **40** of |

## Exercise 12

*For*
(Each preposition or phrase should be used once only.)

| | | |
|---|---|---|
| **1** in search of | **5** in exchange for | **8** on account of |
| **2** in return for | **6** in order to obtain | **9** on behalf of |
| **3** to | **7** in favour of | **10** Regarding |
| **4** during | | |

**Exercise 13**

*Prepositional phrases*

1 frank
2 confused
3 in our favour
4 referred to
5 irrelevant
6 out of control
7 nervous
8 ever
9 friendly
10 gay
11 briefly
12 usually
13 fully
14 richer
15 without result

**Exercise 14**

*Verbs, nouns and adjectives followed by* FOR
(Each word should be used once only.)

1 candidate
2 cure
3 recommend
4 available
5 pray
6 plan
7 reach
8 demand
9 blame
10 sufficient
11 difficult
12 necessary

**Exercise 15**

*Nouns and adjectives followed by* TO
(Each word should be used once only.)

1 danger
2 convenient
3 loyal
4 grateful
5 new
6 marriage
7 reference
8 blind
9 credit
10 available

**Exercise 16**

*Prepositional phrases*

1 together with
2 apart from
3 because of

| 4 together with | 7 as for | 9 because of |
|---|---|---|
| 5 as to | 8 according to | 10 similar to |
| 6 but for | | |

**Exercise 17**

*Pay, pay for*

| 1 pay | 2 pay for | 3 pay for | 4 pay for |
|---|---|---|---|

**Exercise 18**

*Verbs, nouns and adjectives followed by prepositions*

| 1 for | 6 of | 10 for (of) | 14 for | 18 on |
|---|---|---|---|---|
| 2 of | 7 at | 11 from | 15 to | (upon) |
| 3 for | 8 to | 12 in | 16 to | 19 to |
| 4 over (on) | 9 for | 13 to | 17 from | 20 to |
| 5 in | | | | |

**Exercise 19**

*Miscellaneous: difference in meaning*      (MODEL ANSWERS)

1 The first sentence means that the woman *met* Dick *by chance* in the jungle; the second sentence refers to the woman *attacking* Dick in the jungle.
2 The committee members were *in agreement* about holding the meeting in the first sentence, but they were *undecided* about it in the second sentence. The second sentence is thus almost opposite in the meaning to the first sentence.

**3** The road in the first sentence is *in good condition*; in the second sentence the road is *being repaired*.

**4** The first sentence refers to the uselessness of trying to *buy the ownership* of the man's shops; the second sentence refers to the uselessness of trying to *bribe* the man: he owns many shops and is rich.

**5** In sentence (a) the teacher either *excused* several pupils or *allowed* them *to go unpunished*; in sentence (b) the teacher *failed* (or *disappointed*) several pupils, probably when they most needed the teacher's help.

**Exercise 20**

*Due to, owing to*

| | | |
|---|---|---|
| **1** owing to | **5** due to | **8** due to |
| **2** due to | **6** Owing to | **9** due to |
| **3** Owing to | **7** owing to | **10** owing to |
| **4** owing to | | |

**Exercise 21**

*Play*

| | | |
|---|---|---|
| **1** for | **5** on (upon) | **8** up |
| **2** outside | **6** up to | **9** out |
| **3** for (in, against) | **7** out | **10** off against |
| **4** off | | |

**Exercise 22**

*Call*

| | | |
|---|---|---|
| **1** in | **2** away (out) | **3** up |

| 4 out (on) | 7 off | 9 up |
| 5 out | 8 to | 10 on (upon) |
| 6 for | | |

## Exercise 23

*Set*

| 1 out | 6 out (off) | 11 down (out) |
| 2 in | 7 up | 12 aside (by) |
| 3 about | 8 to | 13 up |
| 4 off | 9 off | 14 aside (by) |
| 5 off | 10 forward | 15 down |

## Exercise 24

*Keep*

| 1 keeping back | 5 keep up | 8 kept down |
| 2 kept in | 6 kept in | 9 keep at |
| 3 kept on | 7 keep away from | 10 kept on at |
| 4 keep up | | |

## Exercise 25

*Phrasal verbs*

| 1 respect | 5 steal | 8 destroy |
| 2 happen | 6 support | 9 faint |
| 3 confuse | 7 support | 10 withstand |
| 4 exaggerate | | |

**Exercise 26**

*Down*
(Use each verb once only.)

| | | |
|---|---|---|
| 1 knocked | 8 fell | 15 step |
| 2 knelt | 9 hunt | 16 cools |
| 3 wash | 10 Bend | 17 Pull |
| 4 broke | 11 burnt | 18 closed |
| 5 slow | 12 called | 19 lashed |
| 6 nailing | 13 trample | 20 watered |
| 7 lie | 14 wrote | |

**Exercise 27**

*In*
(Each verb should be used once only.)

| | | |
|---|---|---|
| 1 shut | 6 dropped | 11 settled |
| 2 turns | 7 sunk | 12 Bring |
| 3 come | 8 allowed | 13 stay |
| 4 keeping | 9 locked | 14 rubbing |
| 5 hand | 10 drive | 15 ushered |

**Exercise 28**

*Adverbial particles*

| | | |
|---|---|---|
| 1 away | 4 out | 9 on (back) |
| (along, on) | 5 over (across) | 10 round (around) |
| 2 about | 6 back (on) | 11 down |
| (around, by) | 7 up | 12 off |
| 3 in | 8 out | 13 out |

36

| | | |
|---|---|---|
| **14** out | **28** down | **41** in |
| **15** round (around) | **29** in | **42** up |
| **16** off | **30** out | **43** off |
| **17** up | **31** by (past, on, | **44** over |
| **18** on (way, off) | along) | **45** out (on) |
| **19** Off | **32** beyond | **46** on |
| **20** out | **33** on | **47** on |
| **21** up (out) | **34** out | **48** down |
| **22** up | **35** up | **49** off |
| **23** in | **36** off | **50** out |
| **24** off | **37** up | **51** down |
| **25** on | **38** out | **52** up |
| **26** back | **39** over | **53** out |
| **27** out | **40** out | **54** up |

**Exercise 29**

*Nouns and adjectives followed by prepositions*

| | | |
|---|---|---|
| **1** to | **8** to | **15** for |
| **2** with | **9** to ... for | **16** by |
| **3** for | **10** to | **17** of (about) |
| **4** of | **11** in | **18** on |
| **5** of | **12** for | **19** on (upon) |
| **6** to ... for | **13** to | **20** to |
| **7** for | **14** on (upon) | |

**Exercise 30**

*Verbs followed by prepositions*

| | | |
|---|---|---|
| **1** to | **3** to | **5** X |
| **2** for | **4** from | **6** from |

| | | |
|---|---|---|
| **7** for | **11** for | **16** in |
| **8** X | **12** on (upon) | **17** for |
| **9** with . . . on | **13** from | **18** on (upon) |
|     (about over) | **14** to . . . for | **19** from |
| **10** of | **15** for | **20** from (by) |

## Exercise 31

*Verbs followed by prepositions and particles: difference in meaning*   (MODEL ANSWERS)

| | |
|---|---|
| drive *at* | I don't understand what you are *driving at*: please explain what you mean. |
| drive *off* | *The policeman drove* the crowd *off* and the footballers were left alone. |
| read *up* | 'You ought to *read up* your notes before the examination,' the history teacher told the class. |
| read *into* | He *read into* the poem a deeper meaning than the obvious one. |
| stand *in for* | Joyce got her big chance to act in the play when she *stood in for* the famous actress who was ill. |
| stand *out for* | The union leader *stood out for* an increase in pay before he would allow his men to return to work. |
| care *about* | The proud man *cared* a lot *about* his good reputation. |
| care *for* | Tom's sister *cared for* him when he was ill. |
| fall *for* | Robert soon *fell for* the beautiful Elizabeth and asked her to be his wife. |
| fall *under* | The company now *falls under* the command of Major James Lee. |

**Exercise 32**

*Prepositional phrases containing the noun* HAND

1 on all hands (on every hand)
2 in hand
3 *bitter* hand-to-hand *fighting*
4 in hand
5 with a high hand
6 with a heavy hand
7 hand in hand
8 in hand
9 *has been woven* by hand
10 at hand

**Exercise 33**

*Prepositional phrases containing the noun* HEART

1 by heart
2 nearest her heart
3 *hope* with all my heart
4 heart-to-heart
5 out of heart
6 at heart

**Exercise 34**

*Prepositional phrases: difference in meaning*
(MODEL ANSWERS)

1 *At last*, after many attempts, Mr Brown succeeded in passing his driving-test.
   The dying man was cheerful *to the last*, always making jokes even though he was suffering a great deal.
2 The shy lovers met regularly for seven years: *in the end* they decided to get married.
   It has been raining for weeks *on end*: I last saw the sun two months ago.

3 Mr Lee was rather old to resign and start on a new career *from scratch*.

The sergeant was very strict and always tried to keep his men *up to scratch* so that they would be good soldiers.

4 'I'll come downstairs *in an instant*,' Jane called out: the next moment she was running down the stairs.

'You will not be punished,' the headmaster said. '*In this instance*, you have a good excuse for being late.'

**Exercise 35**

*Phrasal verbs*

1 continued
2 hiding(concealing)
3 recover
4 arrested
5 tired (bored)
6 solved
7 consider (study)
8 happening
9 managing
10 disconnected *me*
11 encouraged (urged) her *husband*
12 confirms (supports)
13 expire
14 (tele) phone *me*
15 died
16 stopped
17 interrupted
18 revived *Mrs Stout*
19 admit
20 postponed

**Exercise 36**

*Phrasal verbs*

1 fell out
2 getting on
3 called up
4 let out
5 owned up
6 cut *her* off
7 taken in
8 turned over
9 let down
10 standing in
11 see off
12 make up
13 getting on for
14 go in for
15 get on

**Exercise 37**

*Run*

1 in poor health (tired and weak)
2 encountered (met)
3 completed (finished)
4 happened to meet (met. . . by chance)
5 collided with (crashed into)
6 print
7 review (go over)
8 amount to (reach)
9 disparage (say unkind things about) *Mrs Green*
10 concerned (occupied) with

**Exercise 38**

*Break*

1 broke out of
2 break up
3 broke out
4 broken down
5 broke down
6 broken through
7 break up
8 broke into
9 broken off
10 break in

**Exercise 39**

*Let*

1 on; reveal (divulge)
2 down; lowered
3 in; admitted
4 in on; reveal (share)
5 off; excused (allowed him to go unpunished)
6 down; fail (disappoint)
7 off; excused
8 in for; become involved in
9 out at; attacked
10 up; diminished

## Exercise 40

*Fall*

| | | |
|---|---|---|
| 1 fell in with | 5 fallen back | 8 fell out |
| 2 fell into | 6 have fallen on | 9 falls under |
| 3 fallen off | 7 fall in | 10 fell through |
| 4 fallen out with | | |

## Exercise 41

*Put*

| | |
|---|---|
| 1 put by (aside) | 9 put on |
| 2 put down | 10 put *me* through |
| 3 put in | 11 put *it* back |
| 4 put out | 12 put about |
| 5 put up with | 13 put *you* out (about) |
| 6 put up | 14 put out |
| 7 put *the weary travellers* up (put up *the . . .*) | 15 putting on |
| 8 put on | 16 put off |

## Exercise 42

*Take in, take up*

| | |
|---|---|
| 1 deceived (cheated) | 6 occupying |
| 2 making smaller | 7 shortening |
| 3 understand (follow) | 8 begun (begun to do) |
| 4 includes | 9 corrected (interrupted) |
| 5 admitted (received) | 10 pursue |

**Exercise 43**

*Verbal collocations with different meanings*
(MODEL ANSWERS)

1 In the first sentence the emperor was *not deceived* by the cunning plans of the generals; in the second sentence the engineer was determined to *ensure* that the bridge was *completed*.

2 *To be run down* in the first sentence means *to be weak, tired or in poor health*; *to run others down* in the second sentence means *to disparage other people*.

3 In the first sentence *break out* means *escape*: the animals escaped from their cages during the fire. The second sentence refers to a fire starting: *break out* is often used with unpleasant things such as wars, fires, diseases and means *begin* or *start*.

   A meeting that is *called off* is *cancelled*. If a man *calls off* his dog from attacking a thief, he diverts or distracts it and thus stops it from attacking the thief.

5 If the quality of food, etc. *goes off*, it *deteriorates*. When a bomb *goes off*, it *explodes*.

6 *Fell out* in sentence (a) means *happened*, while in sentence (b) it means *quarrelled*.

7 A girl who *keeps to herself* is *unsociable* or *retiring*: she does not want to meet people. A woman who *keeps knowledge* (or *a secret*, etc.) *to herself* does not tell anyone else about it.

8 *Come to* in sentence (a) means *amount to*, while in sentence (b) *came to* means *regained consciousness*.

9 The first sentence refers to bandits *stopping and robbing* a stagecoach; the second sentence refers to a dock strike *delaying* the delivery of some goods.

10 If you *turn out* your pockets, you *empty everything out* of them; if you *turn out* to see a football match, etc., you

go out *(leave your house)* for the purpose of seeing the match, etc.

## Exercise 44

*Replacement by prepositional phrases*

| | | | |
|---|---|---|---|
| 1 | in consideration of | 10 | in the pay of |
| 2 | in face of | 11 | within an ace of |
| 3 | on the grounds of | 12 | for the love of |
| 4 | in addition to | 13 | in keeping with |
| 5 | in the hands of | 14 | on the eve of |
| 6 | in lieu of | 15 | by force of |
| 7 | in the power of | 16 | at home with |
| 8 | in charge of | 17 | on the face of it |
| 9 | on the threshold of | 18 | in the region of |

## Exercise 45

*Talk*

1 *Tom* talked back to *his father*
2 *We* talked over the recent ...
3 ... *and* talked *the clerk* down
4 ... *has* talked *me* out of *climbing* ...
5 *Mary* talked away *while* ...

## Exercise 46

*Live*

1 with      2 in      3 on      4 for

Exercise 49

Exercise 47

*Make*

| | | |
|---|---|---|
| 1 for | 5 after | 9 up |
| 2 at (for) | 6 of | 10 away with |
| 3 off with | 7 out | 11 out |
| 4 off | 8 up to | 12 up |

1 They were going to Ipoh.
2 Three bandits did.
3 They stole a horse.
4 The other two bandits soon ran away.
5 They were going to pursue the bandits.
6 The strange man invented it.
7 . . . kill himself (commit suicide).
8 One of the bandits did.

Exercise 48

*Pull*

| | | | | |
|---|---|---|---|---|
| 1 off | 3 over | 4 up | 5 up | 6 down |
| 2 through | | | | |

1 . . . win.
2 Many doctors thought this.
3 It stopped about a hundred yards in front of Jonathan.
4 . . . demolished.

Exercise 49

*Deal*

| | | | | |
|---|---|---|---|---|
| 1 in | 2 by (with) | 3 with | 4 with | 5 with |

1 He does business in wool.
2 He has always behaved fairly to the writer.
3 Several of Mr Blake's business friends did.
4 Most of them concerned the problem of transporting the wool.

**Exercise 50**

*Miscellaneous*

| | | |
|---|---|---|
| 1 to | 25 to | 49 out |
| 2 in | 26 from (out of ) | 50 off |
| 3 in | 27 to | 51 on |
| 4 with | 28 off | 52 about |
| 5 at | 29 down | 53 at |
| 6 at | 30 about | 54 up |
| 7 for | 31 by | 55 to (into) |
| 8 about | 32 off | 56 in |
| 9 of | 33 of | 57 up |
| 10 from (to) | 34 with | 58 of |
| 11 in | 35 on (of ) | 59 from (out of ) |
| 12 from | 36 to (with) | 60 after |
| 13 to | 37 for | 61 from |
| 14 like | 38 out | 62 before |
| 15 in | 39 in | 63 in |
| 16 at | 40 from (out of ) | 64 up to (up onto, |
| 17 of | 41 with | out onto) |
| 18 in | 42 In (Within) | 65 to |
| 19 to | 43 to | 66 of |
| 20 in | 44 out of (out from) | 67 of |
| 21 with | 45 for | 68 out |
| 22 of | 46 of | 69 off |
| 23 in | 47 back (in) | 70 in |
| 24 in | 48 about | 71 out of |

**Exercise 51**

*Miscellaneous*

| | | |
|---|---|---|
| 1 upon | 14 off (away) with | 25 In |
| 2 for | 15 at | 26 for |
| 3 in | 16 like | 27 with |
| 4 to | 17 to | 28 to |
| 5 into | 18 like | 29 upon |
| 6 on (upon) | 19 In | 30 upon (across) |
| 7 through | 20 of | 31 in |
| 8 in (round) | 21 of | 32 up to (with) |
| 9 about (of) | 22 out with | 33 of |
| 10 on | 23 at | 34 over (about) |
| 11 into (across) | (through, over) | 35 from (to) |
| 12 at | 24 before | 36 of |
| 13 of | | |

**Exercise 52**

*Miscellaneous*

| | | |
|---|---|---|
| 1 from | 13 in for | 25 At |
| 2 to | 14 to (into) | 26 out |
| 3 by (along) | 15 down | 27 in |
| 4 to | 16 out (in) | 28 for |
| 5 In | 17 back | 29 into |
| 6 in | 18 off (away) | 30 with |
| 7 off | 19 of | 31 about |
| 8 to | 20 at | 32 at |
| 9 with | 21 in (with) | 33 with |
| 10 in | 22 for | 34 into |
| 11 for | 23 out | 35 in |
| 12 with | 24 on (along) | 36 back |

| | | |
|---|---|---|
| **37** out | **48** on | **58** over |
| **38** from | **49** up to | **59** at |
| **39** out | **50** into | **60** out |
| **40** over | **51** out | **61** off |
| **41** into | **52** for | **62** over |
| **42** in | **53** at | **63** of |
| **43** up | **54** up | **64** of |
| **44** in | **55** out before | **65** for |
| **45** out | **56** for | **66** to |
| **46** on | **57** to | **67** without |
| **47** to | | |

**Exercise 53**

*Miscellaneous*

| | | |
|---|---|---|
| **1** At | **19** in | **37** on |
| **2** up | **20** on (upon) | **38** to |
| **3** with | **21** in | **39** for |
| **4** on | **22** of | **40** of |
| **5** in | **23** by | **41** in |
| **6** out of | **24** from | **42** for |
| **7** into (across) | **25** on | **43** by (near) |
| **8** by | **26** in | **44** of |
| **9** in | **27** of | **45** on (upon) |
| **10** in | **28** out of | **46** on (upon) |
| **11** from | **29** up to | **47** without |
| **12** from | **30** with | **48** after |
| **13** on (in) | **31** for | **49** from |
| **14** for | **32** on | **50** across |
| **15** of | **33** up | **51** to |
| **16** at | **34** out | **52** opposite |
| **17** on | **35** away | **53** for |
| **18** on | **36** in | **54** on |

| | | |
|---|---|---|
| **55** at | **78** for | **100** during |
| **56** of | **79** of | **101** In |
| **57** at | **80** to | **102** for |
| **58** with | **81** at | **103** out of (away |
| **59** at (on) | **82** after | from) |
| **60** for | **83** with | **104** about (over) |
| **61** for | **84** in | **105** of |
| **62** to | **85** of | **106** in |
| **63** for | **86** down to | **107** up |
| **64** out of | **87** by | **108** out |
| **65** down (up, into) | **88** by (to) | **109** about |
| **66** for | **89** out | **110** for |
| **67** at (by) | **90** in | **111** in |
| **68** over | **91** on | **112** in |
| **69** off | **92** up (round) | **113** for |
| **70** on (upon) | **93** down (round) | **114** out |
| **71** over | **94** at | **115** in |
| **72** off | **95** in | **116** of |
| **73** at | **96** with | **117** up |
| **74** by | **97** between | **118** with |
| **75** for | **98** for | **119** off |
| **76** By | **99** with | **120** out with |
| **77** in | | |

# WORKBOOK THREE

## Exercise 1

*Prepositions*

| | | |
|---|---|---|
| 1 on | 10 at . . . among | 19 with |
| 2 in | 11 in . . . by (before) | 20 without |
| 3 over | 12 despite | 21 of . . . on |
| 4 to | 13 for | (about, con- |
| 5 in | 14 in . . . with | cerning) |
| 6 to | 15 on | 22 into . . . for |
| 7 to | 16 on | 23 for |
| 8 under | 17 at (over, for) | 24 for |
| 9 beneath | 18 through | 25 against |

## Exercise 2

*Verbs, nouns and adjectives followed by prepositions*

| | | | | |
|---|---|---|---|---|
| 1 in | 5 on | 9 against | 13 in | 17 of |
| 2 from | 6 with | 10 by | 14 on | 18 of |
| 3 about | 7 upon | 11 with | 15 of | 19 for |
| 4 with | 8 of | 12 at | 16 for | 20 of |

## Exercise 3

*Verbs, nouns, and adjectives followed by prepositions*
(Use each phrase on the right once only.)

| | | | | |
|---|---|---|---|---|
| 1 3 | 5 7 | 9 1 | 13 19 | 17 20 |
| 2 6 | 6 2 | 10 9 | 14 11 | 18 12 |
| 3 5 | 7 10 | 11 15 | 15 18 | 19 14 |
| 4 8 | 8 4 | 12 17 | 16 13 | 20 16 |

## Exercise 4

*Missing preposition + noun + missing preposition*

| | | |
|---|---|---|
| 1 in . . . of | 8 in . . . of | 15 in . . . of |
| 2 in . . . of | 9 in . . . of | 16 in . . . of |
| 3 in . . . of | 10 in . . . of | 17 in . . . for |
| 4 with . . . to | 11 in (during) . . . of | 18 in . . . about (of) |
| 5 in . . . to | 12 in . . . of | 19 in . . . to |
| 6 in . . . with | 13 for . . . of | 20 in . . . of |
| 7 on . . . of | 14 in . . . of | |

## Exercise 5

*Replacement: prepositional phrases*

| | |
|---|---|
| 1 through lack of | 6 in the best part of |
| 2 engaged on | 7 on the grounds of |
| 3 under threat of | 8 to the advantage of |
| 4 because of | 9 in disagreement with |
| 5 friendly with | 10 in view of the possibility of |

## Exercise 6

*Prepositional phrases*

| | |
|---|---|
| 1 undecided | 8 contrary to orders |
| 2 dead | 9 matter-of-fact |
| 3 engaged on a futile task | 10 in every detail |
| 4 in some respects | 11 at one's best |
| 5 offensive | 12 quickly |
| 6 to create a good impression | 13 unimportant |
| 7 attacking | 14 everything considered |

**15** likely
**16** putting it simply
**17** confidentially

**18** with nothing to do
**19** regardless of difficulties
**20** with great success

**Exercise 7**

*Adverbial particles*

**1** in (out)
**2** about
**3** round
**4** out (away, off)
**5** down
**6** out
**7** away
**8** out
**9** away
**10** through (along)
**11** up
**12** on (away)
**13** up
**14** down
**15** up
**16** about (around, by, near)
**17** over

**18** back
**19** out (round)
**20** away (off)
**21** over
**22** on
**23** in
**24** down
**25** in (up)
**26** out
**27** out
**28** out (round)
**29** in (out)
**30** out
**31** on (out)
**32** up
**33** out
**34** out
**35** up

**36** out (round)
**37** on
**38** down
**39** off
**40** on
**41** in
**42** over
**43** off (away)
**44** on (by, past)
**45** down
**46** up
**47** past (by)
**48** off
**49** down
**50** out
**51** up
**52** away

**Exercise 8**

*Replacement: phrasal verbs*

**1** did away with
**2** piling it on

**3** made it up
**4** rang off

**5** got on to
**6** egged *you* on

| 7 rattled off | 10 turned to | 13 came in for |
|---|---|---|
| 8 gone down with | 11 held over | 14 worn out |
| 9 is cut out for | 12 straightened out | 15 ran down |

## Exercise 9

*Tell*

1 by (from)    2 about    3 on    4 on

1 He could recognise that he (the old man) had once been very rich.
2 It began to have a bad effect on him (It began to be too much for him).
3 He asked Jack not to inform against him.

## Exercise 10

*Talk*

| 1 about (of ) | 4 out of | 7 to (with) |
|---|---|---|
| 2 away (on) | 5 down | 8 into |
| 3 over | 6 back to | 9 to |

1 Joan used to, (Joan did).
2 He discussed the whole matter about Fred.
3 He tried to dissuade her from going to the cinema with Fred.
4 She silenced him by talking.
5 He did not wish to persuade Joan's father to punish her.
6 Yes, he did.

**Exercise 11**

*Speak*

| | | |
|---|---|---|
| **1** about (of) | **3** for (against) | **5** before (to) |
| **2** on (about) | **4** against (for) | **6** up |

**Exercise 12**

*Verbs followed by prepositions*

| | | |
|---|---|---|
| **1** for | **12** on (upon) | **21** for |
| **2** in (with) | **13** in . . . from | **22** over |
| **3** into | (out of) | **23** for |
| **4** of | **14** in | **24** for |
| **5** to | **15** on (upon) | **25** with . . . about |
| **6** with | **16** for (with) | **26** for |
| **7** over (at) | **17** for | **27** by |
| **8** for | **18** from . . . on | **28** at |
| **9** to | **19** to | **29** for . . . under |
| **10** on (upon) | **20** of | **30** to (by) |
| **11** out of | | |

**Exercise 13**

*Replacement: verbs followed by prepositions*

| | | |
|---|---|---|
| **1** reckoned on | **6** watched over | **11** scraped through |
| **2** faces on to | **7** hear of | **12** cared for |
| **3** stuck by | **8** sit on | **13** tumble to |
| **4** comes under | **9** rests with | **14** clashed with |
| **5** felt for | **10** put upon | **15** broken with |

## Exercise 14

*Nouns and adjectives followed by prepositions*

| | | |
|---|---|---|
| **1** for | **12** for | **21** for |
| **2** with | **13** about | **22** for |
| **3** for | (concerning, on) | **23** for |
| **4** to | **14** for | **24** of |
| **5** to | **15** on (upon) | **25** to |
| **6** for | **16** for | **26** about |
| **7** in | **17** on (upon) | **27** to |
| **8** of | **18** for | **28** to |
| **9** for | **19** in | **29** on (upon) |
| **10** to | **20** on (upon) | **30** of |
| **11** for | | |

## Exercise 15

*Nouns and adjectives followed by prepositions*

| | |
|---|---|
| **1** reason for | **7** close behind |
| **2** opposed to | **8** very keen on |
| **3** in the habit of producing | **9** indifferent to |
| **4** very inferior to | **10** determined to do |
| **5** revenge oneself upon | **11** take liberties with |
| **6** understanding of | **12** like |

## Exercise 16

*Prepositional phrases*    (MODEL ANSWERS)

**1** In sentence (a) *at large* means *free*, while in sentence (b) *at large* means *generally*: the person's views on education are generally quite sound.

**2** In the first sentence the speaker desires that everything be put back *in order* as it was before; in the second sentence he is asking if it is *suitable* (*all right*) for him to leave the meeting.

**3** The first sentence means that Professor Hill's talk was *too difficult to understand*; the second sentence refers to a junior clerk who complained direct to the chief manager *without asking permission* from, or *without first mentioning the matter* to his immediate superiors.

**4** In sentence (a) five candidates were *not* interviewed in proper succession. In sentence (b) the chairman says that it is *not permissible* or it is *against the rules* to speak more than once during the debate. In sentence (c) the radio won't work because it is *broken*.

**5** The efforts referred to in the first sentence have been *in vain*; the second sentence refers to a servant who prefers to work *free of charge* or *without payment* rather than continue working for the person addressed.

**6** The clever lawyer's services mentioned in sentence (a) were *in great demand*; the shares in sentence (b) are being sold *at more than their nominal value*.

**7** *In time* in the first sentence means *eventually*, while in the second sentence it is used to mean *early enough* or *not late*.

**Exercise 17**

*Except, except for*

| | | |
|---|---|---|
| **1** except for | **5** except for | **8** except |
| **2** except | **6** except | **9** except |
| **3** except for | **7** except for | **10** except |
| **4** except | | |

**Exercise 18**

*Particles following* ALL

| | | |
|---|---|---|
| 1 all in all | 4 all over | 7 all over |
| 2 all in | 5 all in | 8 all up |
| 3 all along | 6 gone all out | |

**Exercise 19**

*Compound words containing prepositions and particles*

| | | | | |
|---|---|---|---|---|
| 1 down | 10 over | 18 up | 26 under | 34 out |
| 2 up | 11 out | 19 by | 27 up | 35 on |
| 3 under | 12 out | 20 before | 28 out | 36 under |
| 4 above | 13 by | 21 up | 29 out | 37 out |
| 5 on | 14 over | 22 up | 30 out | 38 out |
| 6 out | 15 out-of | 23 under | 31 on | 39 forth |
| 7 under | 16 out | 24 over | 32 over | 40 over |
| 8 under | 17 out | 25 over | 33 by | 41 under |
| 9 down | | | | |

**Exercise 20**

*Compound words containing adverbial particles*

| | | | | |
|---|---|---|---|---|
| 1 in | 8 on | 15 back | 22 down | 28 up |
| 2 up | 9 up | 16 back | 23 away | 29 between |
| 3 down | 10 up | 17 to | 24 down | 30 through |
| 4 out | 11 back | 18 off | 25 up | 31 out |
| 5 out | 12 out | 19 off | 26 out | 32 ups |
| 6 down | 13 on | 20 up | 27 out | 33 out |
| 7 up | 14 down | 21 by | (away) | 34 up |

| 35 by  | 39 out | 42 in  | 45 off  | 48 through |
|--------|--------|--------|---------|------------|
| 36 up  | 40 up  | 43 off | 46 up   | 49 off     |
| 37 out | 41 up  | 44 out | 47 down | 50 out     |
| 38 on  |        |        |         |            |

## Exercise 21

*Idiomatic phrases formed from two particles or adverbs*

| 1 out and out          | 9 By the by           |
|------------------------|-----------------------|
| 2 over and over        | 10 out and away       |
| 3 ins and outs         | 11 through and through|
| 4 inside out           | 12 upside down        |
| 5 on and on            | 13 ups and downs      |
| 6 By and by            | 14 down and out       |
| 7 again and again      | 15 off and on         |
| 8 betwixt and between  |                       |

## Exercise 22

*Verbs followed by prepositions*

| 1 emphasised (stressed) | 11 corroded              |
|-------------------------|--------------------------|
| 2 kill (ruin)           | 12 had (encountered)     |
| 3 concerned             | 13 tolerate (endure)     |
| 4 found                 | 14 chosen                |
| 5 evade                 | 15 liked                 |
| 6 attack                | 16 ignored (disregarded) |
| 7 expected              | 17 betrayed              |
| 8 squandered (spent)    | 18 need (want)           |
| 9 passed                | 19 expects               |
| 10 finished             | 20 attacked              |

**Exercise 23**

*Combinations with* TO BE

1 ... he's late bringing the milk ....
2 ... he's competing against very great odds.
3 ... he's playing his old tricks again.
4 ... Mrs Smith is already well enough to get up and do things.
5 What's happening? (What's the matter?)
6 ... she's always nagging (finding fault with) him.
7 His son has been very pleased with himself (... been behaving in a very conceited way) ever since ....
8 'She's free (not on duty) ....'
9 How many people are in favour of (... people support) the ....?
10 ... were intent on having (were determined to have) a ....
11 ... isn't much (very) good.
12 ... meeting is (has) finished.
13 ... meeting is (has been) cancelled.
14 You're in trouble!
15 He's so poor that he can't afford even a cheap watch.
16 'I don't feel able (I'm not fit) to make a journey ....'
17 ... is it (has it been) published (is it on sale in the shops) yet?
18 You're very much mistaken (You're completely wrong) in ....
19 ... is on friendly (very good) terms with the mayoress ....
20 'You've had all the time you are allowed: you must leave ...' ('It is time for you to leave ...')
21 It's the responsibility of all of us ....
22 ... I've entered for (My name is written down for) the ....
23 ... she's too good to be so dishonest.
24 ... I'm not taking part in it.

**Exercise 24**

*Replacement: phrasal verbs*

| | |
|---|---|
| 1 set up | 8 catching on |
| 2 walked out on | 9 boiled over |
| 3 pick up *John and Mary at* | 10 taken over |
| *ten-thirty* | 11 cut up |
| 4 ruled out | 12 dressed *us* down |
| 5 put up | 13 drop off |
| 6 get down | 14 looked *us* up and down |
| 7 ran on | 15 Shut up |

**Exercise 25**

*Phrasal verbs* (MODEL ANSWERS)

1 The speaker in sentence (a) is asking how Mr Lee is *managing* or *what progress he is making*; the speaker in sentence (b) says that Mr Lee is *getting quite old*.

2 *Lashed out* in sentence (a) means *struck out* or *hit out*, while in sentence (b) it means that the students decided to *spend their money recklessly* or *lavishly*.

3 The fire in sentence (a) *began to blaze again* or *burst into flames*; in sentence (b) *burnt up* is used transitively to refer to the man *destroying* the old newspapers *by burning* them.

4 *Cast off* in the first sentence refers to knitting: Mrs Jones *finished off* a piece of knitting *by slipping the stitches one by one off the needles and securing them to make a proper edge*. *Cast off* in the second sentence refers to the sailors *throwing off the rope holding their boat to the shore*.

5 The armed forces referred to in the first sentence have

*deserted* the king. In the second sentence the speaker's cares *left him* when he set off on his walking holiday.

6 The speaker's watch in sentence (a) *won't work* or *has stopped working*; in sentence (b) the speaker wants to stay at home to *get* his things *ready* or *put* them *all together in a case.*

7 *Wrapped up in* in the first sentence means *involved in, related to* or *dependent on*; in the second sentence *wrapped up in* means *completely absorbed in*.

8 Mr Mouse *withdrew from* the business referred to in sentence (a); in sentence (b) the people concerned *began to walk more quickly*.

9 When the speaker in the first sentence *understood* why John was laughing, he laughed too. The second sentence tells us that wigs seem to have *become popular* with women in many countries.

10 The scheme referred to in the first sentence did not *produce the desired result*; the hotel bill mentioned in the second sentence *was calculated* at £7 each.


**Exercise 26**

*Replacement: prepositional phrases*
(Use each phrase once only.)

| | | | |
|---|---|---|---|
| 1 | in a fix | 10 | By the way |
| 2 | At first sight | 11 | under your nose |
| 3 | in bad repair | 12 | to no purpose |
| 4 | To some degree | 13 | at any price |
| 5 | at fault | 14 | out of your senses |
| 6 | in a rush | 15 | at your own risk |
| 7 | on time | 16 | in no time |
| 8 | in particular | 17 | at close quarters |
| 9 | of note | 18 | in progress |

19 without scathe            21 for the best
20 For a spell

**Exercise 27**

*Prepositional phrases: the same noun in different colloca-tions*   (MODEL ANSWERS)

1a The schoolboys kept strictly *in line* while they walked along the corridor.

b 'This painting interests me: it's just *in my line*,' the art-collector said.

2a The boys put up their hands and each boy answered a question *in turn*.

b 'This piece of meat has been cooked *to a turn*: it's just right,' Mr Lee said.

3a Do everything I told you, but *above all* don't tell any-one our secret.

b That horse did win: you were right in your guess *after all*.

4a Please wait: I'll be ready *in a minute*.

b John arrived at eight o'clock *to the minute* — not a moment before and not a moment after.

5a The scientists were working *against time* to get the rocket ready.

b The animals entered the ark two *at a time*.

6a Although Tom was living in Australia, *in spirit* he was often at home with his parents in Hong Kong.

b James was *in low spirits* after he had failed in the examination.

7a You were guilty *in part* because you should have been more careful.

b Mr Brown took the joke against himself *in good part* and laughed loudly.

**8a** Short dresses are now *in fashion* again: you must buy some.

**b** Lee mended my watch *in a fashion*: it goes but it never keeps the correct time.

**9a** You must consider this poem *as a whole* — not line by line.

**b** *On the whole*, Ann has worked very hard this term.

**10a** I have finished at that firm *for good*: I shall never work there again.

**b** Your meeting with Mr Green is *to the good*: he may be able to help you some day.

**Exercise 28**

*Nouns and adjectives followed by prepositions*

| | | |
|---|---|---|
| **1** at | **11** for | **21** against |
| **2** with | **12** in | **22** for |
| **3** for . . . to (over) | **13** to | **23** of |
| **4** to | **14** with | **24** of |
| **5** of | **15** with | **25** for . . . to |
| **6** for | **16** for | **26** to |
| **7** to . . . for | **17** of | **27** with |
| **8** in | **18** to | **28** for |
| **9** for | **19** with . . . to | **29** with |
| **10** of | **20** from (to) . . . of | **30** from |

**Exercise 29**

*Answer*

| | | | | |
|---|---|---|---|---|
| **1** for | **3** to | **5** to | **7** to | **8** up to |
| **2** back | **4** for | **6** up | | |

1 He realised that the writer could not account for the six watches.
2 He said that it seemed quite obvious why he did not declare them. (His retort was: 'It seems quite obvious, doesn't it?')
3 He was responsible for a child whom he was supposed to meet.
4 Housman was the writer.
5 ... physically very like (the same as) the man described in the file.
6 He could not reply to even half of them.


**Exercise 30**

*Bring*
(Use each sentence in Section B once only.)

| | | | | |
|---|---|---|---|---|
| **1** 5 | **4** 2 | **7** 3 | **9** 12 | **11** 7 |
| **2** 11 | **5** 4 | **8** 10 | **10** 6 | **12** 9 |
| **3** 8 | **6** 1 | | | |


**Exercise 31**

*Carry*

| | | | | |
|---|---|---|---|---|
| **1** on | **3** out | **5** away | **6** on | **7** off |
| **2** away | **4** through | | | |

1 She was flirting with Joe Higgs.
2 Yes, he did; he said that he was determined to do it.
3 His determination to beat Joe sustained him.
4 He continued as if nothing had happened.
5 He won the coveted trophy for the race. (He won the race.)

**Exercise 32**

*Come*

1  to; come to = reached
2  at; came at = attacked
3  to; come to = amount to
4  to; came to terms = made an agreement
5  into; came into = inherited
6  by; come by = obtain (acquire)
   (across; come across = happen to find)
7  to; come to the headmaster's knowledge = become known to the headmaster
8  of; come of age (in English law) = reach the age of 21
9  under; came under the influence of = was influenced by
10 under; come under = be under the authority of
11 off; Come off it = Stop it (Stop speaking or behaving as you are doing)
12 to; came to blows = began fighting
13 across (upon); came across (upon) = found by chance (chanced on)
14 over; came over me = influenced me (took possession of my senses)

**Exercise 33**

*Come*

1  came to (round)
2  came back
3  come up with
4  come off
5  coming up
6  come off
7  come down
8  come in
9  come on
10 came about
11 coming on (along)
12 come forward

| | |
|---|---|
| **13** come out | **19** came out |
| **14** come through (out) | **20** came under (up against) |
| **15** come out | **21** came round |
| **16** came out with | **22** coming on (up) |
| **17** did not come up to | **23** come over (round) |
| **18** came out | **24** comes up |

## Exercise 34

*Cut*

| | |
|---|---|
| **1** felled | **8** interrupted |
| **2** suitable to be | **9** swung (moved quickly |
| **3** killed | across) in front of it |
| **4** cut . . . into pieces | **10** killed |
| **5** stop | **11** destroyed |
| **6** isolated | **12** intercept *the others* |
| **7** reduce | |

## Exercise 35

*Do*

| | | | | |
|---|---|---|---|---|
| **1** without | **3** in (into) | **5** out of | **7** for | **8** for |
| **2** by | **4** with | **6** for | | |

| | |
|---|---|
| **1** dispensed with | **6** . . . who keeps my house |
| **2** . . . *always* treated *me well* | clean, will . . . . |
| **3** . . . *all* translate *the passage* | **7** . . . *made it* serve as *a* |
| into *Chinese* | *shower* |
| **4** . . . *I* want *a cold drink* | **8** . . . *would* kill *anyone* |
| **5** . . . was deprived of *her* | |
| *share* | |

**Exercise 36**

*Do*

1 restored (repaired, redecorated)
2 cheat (get the better of)
3 paint
4 worn out (exhausted)
5 tidy (clear up)
6 fastened
7 exhausted (worn out)
8 tie up

**Exercise 37**

*Draw*

| | | |
|---|---|---|
| 1 on | 7 out | 13 down |
| 2 out | 8 back | 14 up |
| 3 out | 9 for | 15 from |
| 4 up | 10 away | 16 in |
| 5 in (up) | 11 from | 17 up |
| 6 into | 12 out | |

1 He withdrew fifty pence.
2 . . . stopped in the middle of the road outside the bank.
3 He tried to induce him to talk.
4 He suggested that the three boys should cast lots.
5 The writer (i.e. John) did.
6 The press would criticise them a lot.
7 He assumed a rather stiff attitude.
8 The fourth man said that he was enticed (inveigled) into joining the others in the bank robbery.

**Exercise 38**

*Give*

1 give in

2 given up

3 given out
4 giving away (out)
5 given up (over)
6 gave out
7 gave off (out, forth)
8 gave on to
9 Give over (up)
10 gave in
11 gave out
12 given yourself away
13 given herself up to
14 given away

## Exercise 39

*Hold*

1 hold back
2 hold out
3 hold up (out)
4 held up
5 hold to
6 hold out
7 held up
8 Hold on
9 hold off
10 held over
11 held back
12 hold down
13 hold off
14 hold forth
15 hold with

## Exercise 40

*Knock*
(Use each sentence in Section B once only.)

| | | | | | | | | | |
|---|---|---|---|---|---|---|---|---|---|
| 1 | 8 | 4 | 6 | 7 | 2 | 9 | 11 | 11 | 12 |
| 2 | 5 | 5 | 1 | 8 | 3 | 10 | 4 | 12 | 7 |
| 3 | 10 | 6 | 9 | | | | | | |

## Exercise 41

*Lay*

1 out
2 up (by, aside)
3 on
4 out
5 off
6 up
7 down
8 off
9 on
10 off
11 about
12 on
13 out

1 They knew that Mr Robinson had saved a lot of money.
2 They thought that he was exaggerating.
3 They were discharged temporarily.
4 He kept it in the garage and did not use it.
5 It took Mr Robinson four months to have the electricity supplied to his new house.
6 He told Mr Robinson to take a long rest.
7 He was soon knocked unconscious.

## Exercise 42

*Pass*

1 ... *easily* pass for *a famous diplomat.*
2 *He completely* passed over *the main* ....
3 *Mr Smith* passed off *the entire* ....
4 ... *is* passing through *hard times.*
5 ... *stomach-ache* passed off *yet?*
6 *Miss Brown* passed herself off as *a duchess* ....
7 ... *will* pass out *next week.*
8 ... *concert* passed off *very successfully.*
9 *Edward* passed *the counterfeit coin* off *at* ....
10 ... *schoolgirls* passed out *when* ....
11 ... *grandfather* passed away *last week.*
12 *please* pass *the box of chocolates* back *to me* ....

## Exercise 43

*Pay*   (MODEL ANSWERS)

1 One day I shall *pay* Tom *back* for the nasty trick he played on me.

**2** Has Mr Brown *paid back* the ten dollars he borrowed from you last week?

**3** Poor Mr Smithson has *paid out* £50 this month in repair bills for his old car.

(Note: *pay out* is not used with very small amounts.)

**4** The sailors *paid out* (*away*) the rope until the ship began to move away from the quayside.

**5** I'm still waiting to get back the rest of the money I lent Ann. Do you think she'll ever *pay up*?

**6** Mr Robinson *paid* his servant *off* and sent him away after he had caught him stealing food.

## Exercise 44

*Pick*

**1** out; recognise (distinguish from others in the group)
**2** up; acquired (bought at a bargain price)
**3** up; collect (come to take you with me in my car, etc.)
**4** off; shoot one by one
**5** up; chance to learn (happen to find out)
**6** on; single out to torment
**7** up; improved (recovered her strength)
**8** out; chose (selected)
**9** up; rescued
**10** up; lift up

## Exercise 45

*Put*

**1** put by (aside, away)
**2** put back
**3** put forward (up)
**4** put . . . down for
**5** put in
**6** putting it on
**7** put . . . through
**8** put out
**9** put . . . up to
**10** put up (forward)
**11** put on

| | | |
|---|---|---|
| 12 put ... off | 23 put off | 34 put across |
| 13 put ... down to | 24 put in | (over) |
| 14 put in | 25 put away | 35 put away |
| 15 put down | 26 put about | 36 put out |
| 16 put out | 27 put away | 37 put up |
| 17 put up | 28 Put ... aside | 38 put up |
| 18 put upon (on) | 29 put in for | 39 put back |
| 19 put off (out) | 30 put on | 40 put up |
| 20 put about | 31 put ... off | 41 put in |
| 21 put on | 32 put out | 42 put up with |
| 22 put ... out | 33 put up | |
| (about) | | |

## Exercise 46

*Stand*

| | | | | |
|---|---|---|---|---|
| 1 on (upon) | 3 out | 5 down | 7 up to | 9 out |
| 2 in with | 4 for | 6 up for | 8 over | 10 by |

1 He sometimes suspected that Wills had a secret agreement with the opponents of the Party.
2 He was prepared to retire (withdraw) and not be considered for Parliament.
3 He supported George.
4 He felt that George could withstand the strain of an election better than Wills.
5 It would be postponed.
6 They might refuse to support (They might oppose) Wills for a short time.

## Exercise 47

*Take*

| | | |
|---|---|---|
| 1 with | 2 out | 3 off |

| | | |
|---|---|---|
| **4** to | **10** out of | **16** off |
| **5** on | **11** for | **17** on |
| **6** on (upon) | **12** up by | **18** up with |
| **7** down | **13** on | **19** out |
| **8** on | **14** in | **20** in |
| **9** back | **15** into | **21** after |

1 He was very much attracted to her (He liked her very much).
2 He was mimicking (imitating) several famous people.
3 No, he did not.
4 He had threatened to fight George.
5 He was very much upset.
6 It made them exhausted (It exhausted them).
7 He knew that they would not employ him.
8 He had deceived George (He had tricked George into giving him money).
9 He thinks George ressembles him (the writer).

**Exercise 48**

*Throw*    (MODEL ANSWERS)

1 Mr Jones began to devote all his energy to improving . . . .
2 The shopkeeper gave Ann a roll of film with the camera (gave . . . without demanding extra payment).
3 The fault delayed the rescue . . . .
4 The novelist suggested many ideas . . . .
5 The passengers were being sick (*to throw up* = to vomit).
6 All Bill's suggestions were rejected by . . . .
7 He resigned his job.
8 The criminal said that he would trust to the mercy of the court.

9 The teacher occasionally interrupted me with a few casual questions.

10 I couldn't manage to get rid of (lose) the man.

## Exercise 49

*Turn*

| | | |
|---|---|---|
| 1 on (upon, against) | 8 out (away) | 15 out |
| 2 to | 9 over | 16 in |
| 3 on (upon) | 10 to | 17 down |
| 4 out | 11 up | 18 out (off) |
| 5 upside down | 12 on (upon) | 19 up |
| 6 down | 13 up | 20 away |
| 7 up at (to) | 14 over | 21 out (into) |

1 He suddenly became hostile towards them.
2 They went to Mr Marks to ask for some advice.
3 They had rejected it.
4 They expelled him (They sent him out).
5 They went away and thought about (considered) the problem.
6 He said that it depended upon John's support.
7 He said he was going to go to bed.
8 They could not gain admission because it was crowded.
9 Mr Marks did.

## Exercise 50

*Out*

| | | |
|---|---|---|
| 1 camp | 3 Fall | 5 pulled |
| 2 come | 4 sit | 6 stick |

7 Rinse (Wash)
8 tired (worn)
9 Look (Watch)
10 living
11 Cut

12 make
13 took (pulled)
14 last (hold)
15 threw
16 eat (dine)

17 sorted (threw)
18 cried (called, shouted)
19 blotted
20 bale (bail)

**Exercise 51**

*Off*

1 turn
2 finished
3 palming
4 laughed
5 putting
6 went (passed)
7 got

8 working
9 write
10 Finish (Rule)
11 put
12 came
13 showing
14 roped (cordoned)

15 dozed
16 left
17 cried
18 pensioned
19 paid;
20 selling

**Exercise 52**

*Up*

1 showed
2 keep
3 clears
4 taken
5 made (thought)
6 built
7 grow
8 brightened (cheered)

9 end (finish)
10 catch
11 leading (working)
12 booked
13 ran
14 crops (comes, turns)
15 kicked

16 Cheer
17 hang
18 blow
19 looking (picking)
20 hushed

**Exercise 53**

*Combinations with* TO BE

1 . . . 's on at
2 . . . 's off
3 . . . will be along
4 . . . 's down on
5 . . . 'm out of
6 . . . was with
7 . . . was through

8 . . . 're with (for, behind)
9 . . . were on to
10 . . . 's after
11 . . . 're off (away)
12 . . . was down
13 . . . are down for
14 . . . 's up in

**Exercise 54**

*Replacement: phrasal verbs*
(Use each phrasal verb once only.)

1 fallen behind with
2 hit it off
3 fed up with
4 have it out with

5 flared up
6 Buzz off
7 barked out
8 run away with

9 slipped up
10 stick out for
11 cottoned on to
12 pushed off

**Exercise 55**

*Verbs followed by prepositions*

1 in
2 about (to)
3 in
4 at
5 on (upon)
6 in (through)
7 to
8 on (upon)

9 for
10 with
11 on (upon)
12 with
13 with
14 for
15 with
16 against

17 on (upon)
18 on (upon) . . .
   between
19 in
20 on (upon) . . .
   through
21 into
22 on (upon)

| | | |
|---|---|---|
| **23** with | **26** out of | **29** into |
| **24** on (upon) | **27** on | **30** to |
| **25** on | **28** for | |

**Exercise 56**

*Nouns and adjectives followed by prepositions*

| | | |
|---|---|---|
| **1** for | **11** of | **21** with |
| **2** with | **12** for | **22** with |
| **3** for | **13** for | **23** at |
| **4** for | **14** for | **24** in |
| **5** with | **15** for | **25** for . . . on |
| **6** of | **16** in . . . at (in) | **26** to |
| **7** for | **17** to | **27** for |
| **8** with | **18** in . . . from | **28** against (from) |
| **9** of | **19** for . . . to | **29** for |
| **10** on (upon) | **20** of . . . for | **30** of |

**Exercise 57**

*Miscellaneous*

| | | |
|---|---|---|
| **1** up | **10** up to | **19** for |
| **2** off (out) on | **11** over (above) | **20** for |
| **3** for | **12** out in | **21** about |
| **4** with | **13** of | **22** on (upon) |
| **5** of | **14** across (over) | **23** up |
| **6** by (at, before) | **15** in | **24** out |
| **7** in | **16** at | **25** to |
| **8** of | **17** of | **26** of |
| **9** for | **18** of | **27** to |

28 Up
29 up
30 at
31 to
32 down
33 over
34 of
35 with
36 for
37 at
38 on
39 off
40 at
41 before (by)
42 up

43 to
44 down
45 of
46 on
47 out (off) by
48 of
49 of
50 about (of)
51 up
52 in
53 over in
54 up for
55 to
56 before (by, at)

57 down
58 behind
59 on
60 out
61 up for
62 With
63 about (around)
64 on
65 after
66 up with
67 out
68 in
69 of
70 up (out)

**Exercise 58**

*Miscellaneous*

1 in (inside, down)
2 of
3 off
4 without
5 in
6 to
7 about
8 in
9 of
10 into
11 in (inside)
12 at
13 of
14 for

15 for
16 for
17 Before
18 under
19 down at
20 out
21 of
22 up
23 round
24 in
25 through After(In)
26 by
27 in (inside)
28 of

29 on
30 In (Under)
31 off
32 about
33 through
34 of
35 from
36 of
37 in
38 at
39 over
40 at
41 in
42 For

| | | |
|---|---|---|
| 43 on | 62 on (upon) | 81 to |
| 44 up against | 63 at | 82 in (inside) |
| 45 on | 64 down | 83 by |
| 46 down | 65 up with | 84 on (upon) |
| 47 in | 66 to | 85 on |
| 48 down | 67 through | 86 in |
| 49 under (by) | 68 At | 87 in |
| 50 against | 69 of | 88 to (on to) |
| 51 in | 70 in | 89 from (out of) |
| 52 out After | 71 at | 90 into |
| 53 through (down) | 72 of | 91 after |
| 54 for | 73 through | 92 of |
| 55 to (round) | 74 beyond | 93 to |
| 56 with | 75 back | 94 in |
| 57 off | 76 of | 95 to |
| 58 to (round) | 77 for (with) | 96 away |
| 59 through | 78 at | 97 to |
| 60 for | 79 of | 98 up |
| 61 at | 80 by | 99 with |

**Exercise 59**

*Miscellaneous*

| | | |
|---|---|---|
| 1 to | 11 with | 20 to |
| 2 off | 12 out | 21 to |
| 3 got out | 13 around (about, | 22 with |
| 4 at (outside, near) | up) | 23 make out |
| 5 in | 14 away | 24 for |
| 6 of | 15 from | 25 at |
| 7 to | 16 in | 26 in |
| 8 to | 17 of | 27 be put down to |
| 9 up (down) | 18 on (upon) | (be explained |
| 10 over (from) | 19 with | by) |

28 from
29 on
30 of
31 at (around, round)
32 in (inside)
33 by
34 from (out of)
35 at
36 to
37 set about
38 over
39 bring down
40 out (away, off) without
41 After
42 on
43 to (into)
44 for
45 of
46 From

47 by (near)
48 towards
49 like
50 with
51 of
52 by
53 with (by)
54 for
55 cut out for
56 at
57 at
58 in
59 away
60 for
61 at
62 on (over)
63 on
64 out
65 to
66 onto
67 of

68 of
69 ran into (ran came across, came upon)
70 for
71 up with
72 before
73 to
74 to (into)
75 off
76 up
77 before
78 taken off
79 of
80 died away
81 in
82 call on me (come round, come over)
83 on
84 at

**Exercise 60**

*Miscellaneous*

1 in
2 of
3 with
4 to
5 at
6 of
7 by
8 down

9 of
10 in
11 of
12 with
13 until
14 of
15 on (upon)
16 At

17 on
18 of
19 out of
20 for
21 put off
22 at (by)
23 of
24 in

25 of

26 Fall in

27 at

28 of

29 at

30 of

31 under

32 against

33 in

34 fall in with

35 join up

36 about (round, out)

37 flared up

38 down

39 gave himself up to

40 of

41 against

42 stand up to

43 of

44 to

45 in

46 into

47 of

48 got on with

49 on (upon, over)

50 On (Upon, After)

51 of (about)

52 put forward

53 at

54 for

55 for

56 at

57 up

58 for

59 out

60 of (in)

61 held back (hung back)

62 about

63 of

64 to

65 for

66 In

67 in

68 with

69 of

70 to

71 on (upon)

72 from

73 came about (turned out)

74 took up

75 of

76 to

77 in

78 came up to

79 of

80 for

81 of

82 among (amongst)